DO YOU KNOW?

Level 1

3D PRINTING

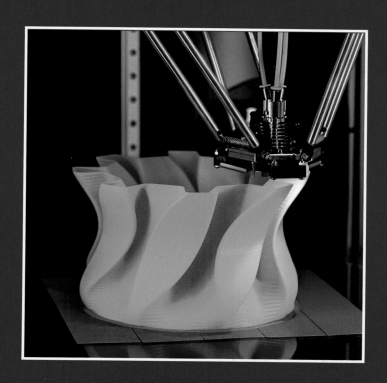

Written by Catherine Saunders
Series Editor: Nick Coates
Designed by Dynamo Limited

LADYBIRD BOOKS

UK | USA | Canada | Ireland | Australia
India | New Zealand | South Africa

Ladybird Books Ltd is part of the Penguin Random House group of companies
whose addresses can be found at global.penguinrandomhouse.com.
www.penguin.co.uk   www.puffin.co.uk   www.ladybird.co.uk

Penguin
Random House
UK

First published 2022
001

Printed in China

The authorized representative in the EEA is Penguin Random House Ireland,
Morrison Chambers, 32 Nassau Street, Dublin D02 YH68

A CIP catalogue record for this book is available from the British Library

ISBN: 978-0-241-55941-3

All correspondence to:
Ladybird Books
Penguin Random House Children's
One Embassy Gardens, 8 Viaduct Gardens, London SW11 7BW

Contents

New words

3D

doctor

flat
(adjective)

hard

idea

layer

machine

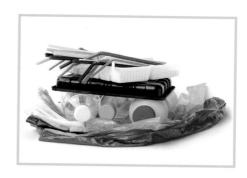

plastic

printer / print
(noun) / (verb)

soft

strong

thing

What is a 3D printer?

Lots of people have **printers**. A printer is a **machine**. A **3D** printer makes 3D **things**.

3D things are not **flat**.

This is a printer. It makes flat pictures on paper.

paper

This is a 3D-printed thing.

💭 THINK!

Draw a picture of a toy you like.
Put the picture next to the toy. Which is 3D?

How old is 3D printing?

Printing is very old, but 3D printing is new.

1030 · 1050 · 1060 · · 1440 · 1460 · · 1800 · 1810 · 1820 · 1830 · 1840 · 1850

1040 AD
Bi Sheng
printing press

1452 AD
Gutenberg's
printing press

1814 AD
Koenig
steam press

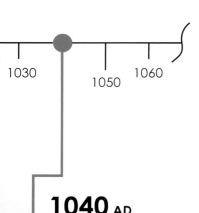

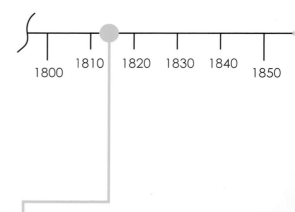

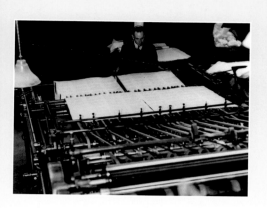

1905 AD
Miehle Verticle press

2002 AD
Full-colour printer

0 1880 1890 1900 1910 1920 1930 1940 1950 1960 1970 1980 2000 2010 203

1990 AD
Dot matrix
black-and-white printer

NOW
Modern 3D printer

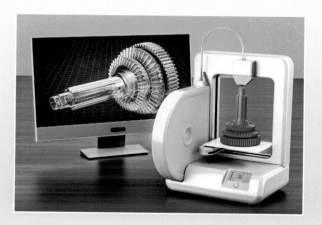

📖 FIND OUT!

Use books or the internet to find out about a machine
you use every day. Whose idea is it? How old is it?

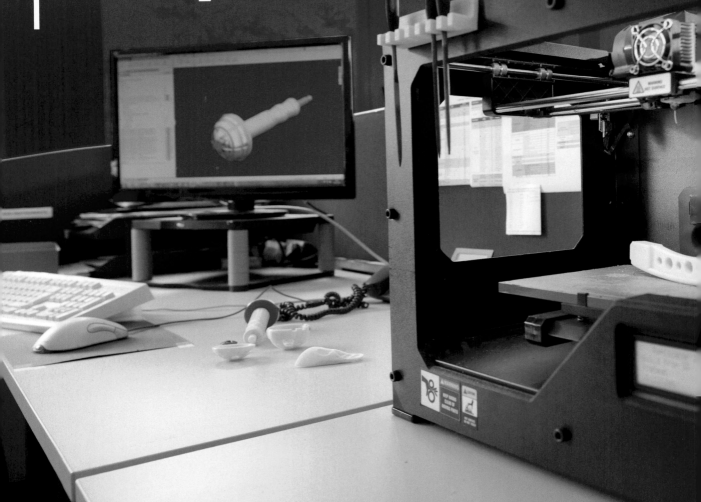

How do you 3D print?

You can draw your **idea** on a computer.

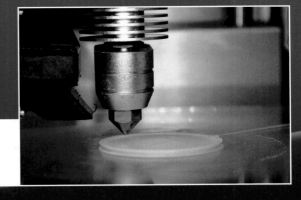

You can send your idea to the 3D printer.

The 3D printer makes lots of **layers**. The layers are hot **plastic**.

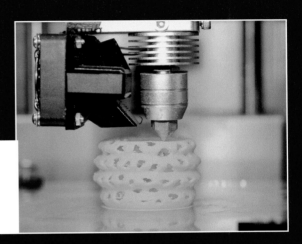

Now the plastic is cold. Cold plastic is **hard**.

▶ WATCH!

Watch the video (see page 32).
Look at this 3D printer! It makes lots of layers.
What thing does it make?

Can you 3D print big things?

Some 3D printers are very big! They make big things.

This bridge is very big. Can you see the layers?

You can 3D print big boats!

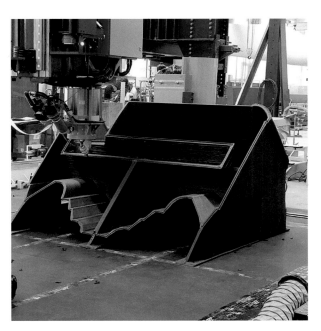

This is a very big 3D printer.

📖 FIND OUT!

Use books or the internet to find out about 3D-printed things in your country.

Can you 3D print small things?

Some 3D printers can make very small things. You cannot see them with your eyes. You can see them with a microscope.

This is a thumb. Can you see the elephant? No, it is too small!

thumb

microscope

elephant

Now can you see the elephant?

THINK!

Can you think of three animals that are smaller than your thumb?

What can you 3D print with?

You can 3D print with plastic, metal and concrete.

Hot plastic is **soft**. It makes layers. Then the plastic is cold and hard!

You can 3D print with metal, too. Hot metal is soft. Cold metal is hard.

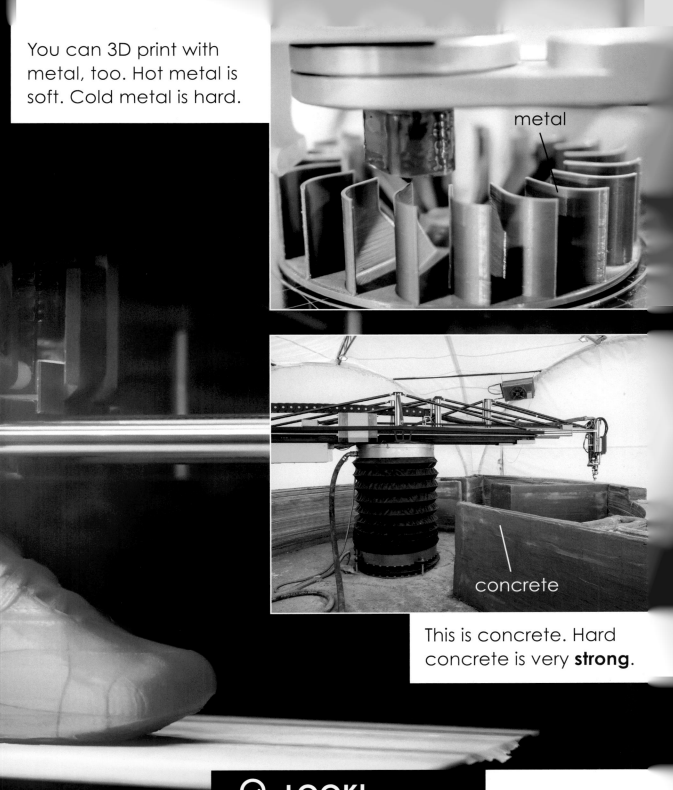

metal

concrete

This is concrete. Hard concrete is very **strong**.

🔍 **LOOK!**

Look at the pages. Can you see the shoe? Is it made with plastic, metal or concrete?

How do you 3D print food?

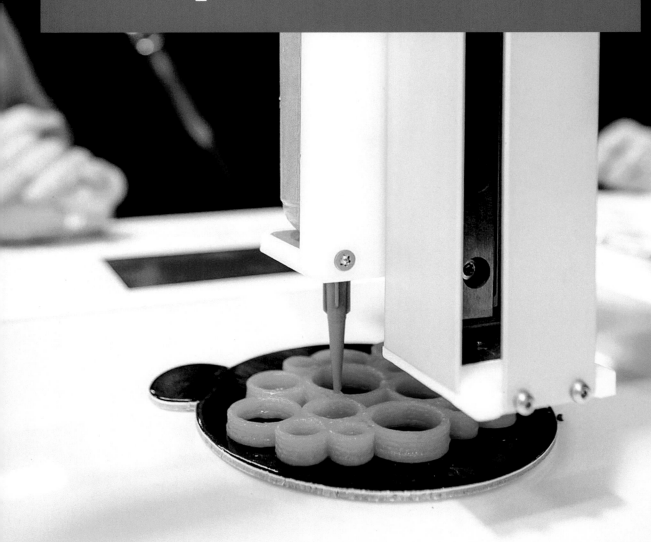

You can put food in some 3D printers.

You can 3D print lots of chocolates.

You can 3D print sweets.

This 3D printer makes great food.

 **THINK!**

When chocolate is hot, is it hard or soft?
Do you want to eat food from a 3D printer?

Do astronauts have 3D printers?

This is the International Space Station. Six astronauts can live here.

There is a 3D printer on the International Space Station. Astronauts can print things.

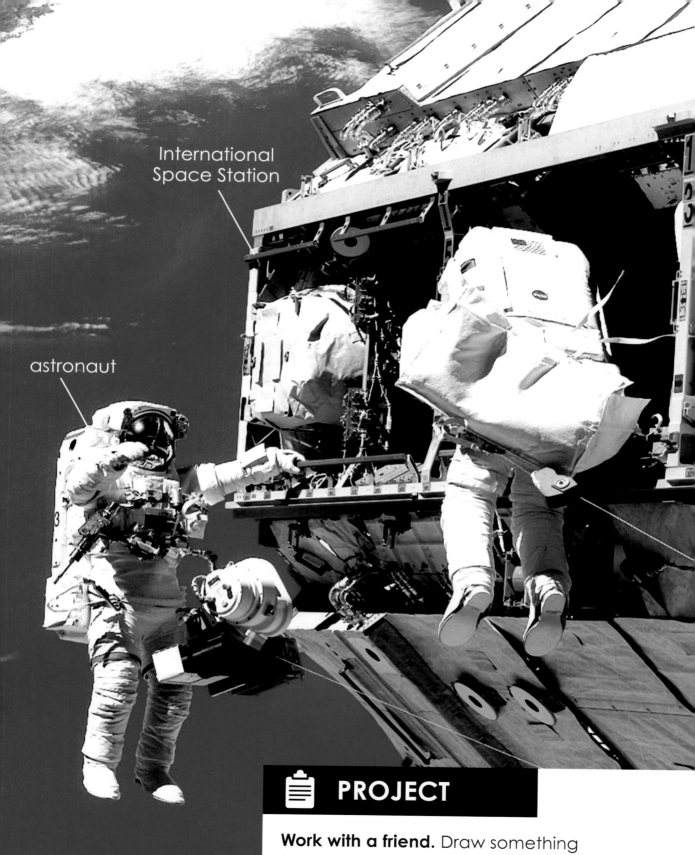

International
Space Station

astronaut

📋 PROJECT

Work with a friend. Draw something
for astronauts to use. Label it!
What is it? What does it do?

How do 3D printers help us?

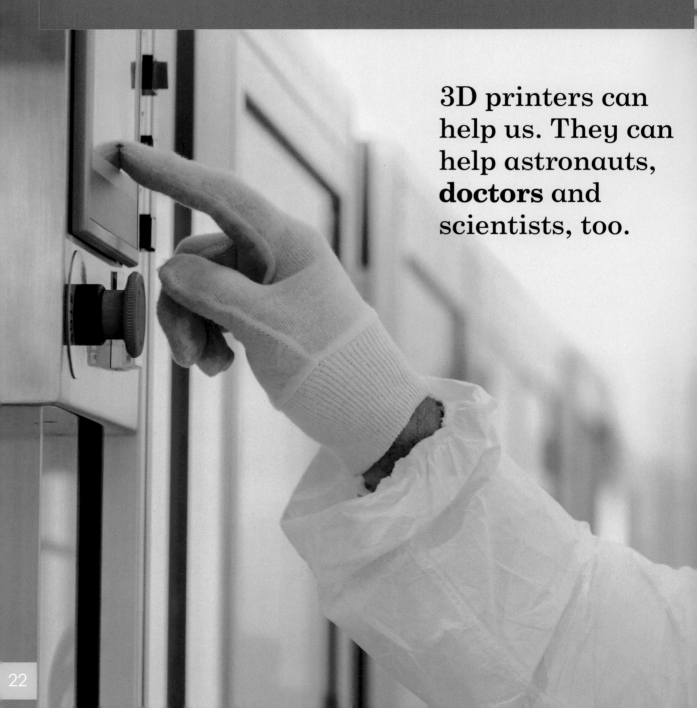

3D printers can help us. They can help astronauts, **doctors** and scientists, too.

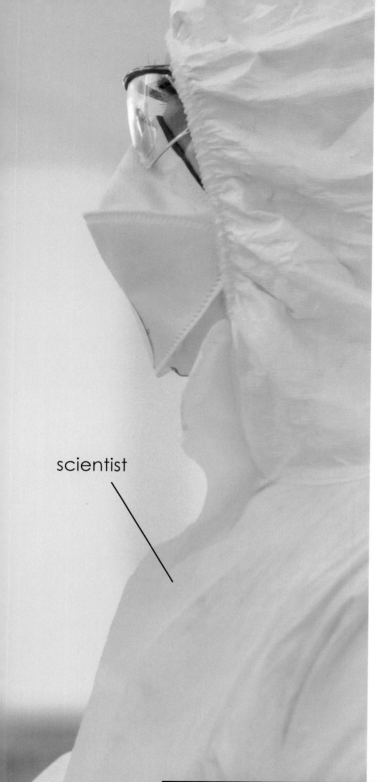

scientist

You can 3D print at home.

You can send ideas to friends. They can 3D print the ideas.

 **FIND OUT!**

Use books or the internet to find out how 3D printing helps doctors and scientists.

Can you 3D print parts of a body?

We can 3D print parts of the body.

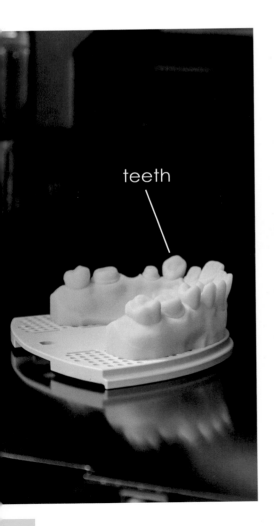

teeth

We can 3D print new teeth.

We can 3D print an arm.

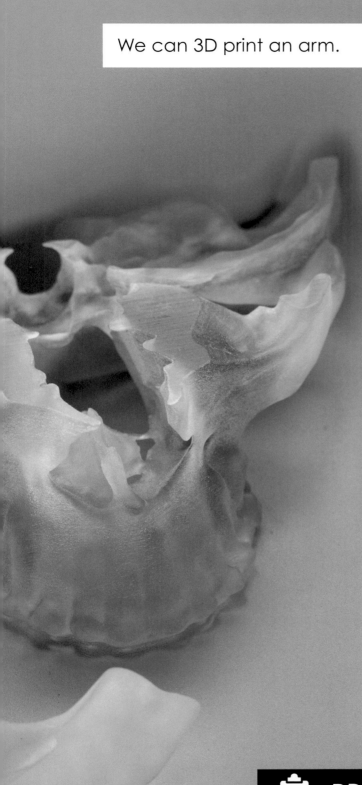

3D-printed arm

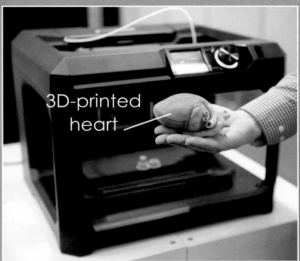

3D-printed heart

We cannot give people a 3D-printed heart today. Maybe we can tomorrow.

 **PROJECT**

Watch the video (see page 32).
What other things can doctors 3D print?

Does 3D printing help animals?

We can help animals with 3D printing.

This dog has a 3D-printed jaw.

This bird has a 3D-printed beak.

beak

bird

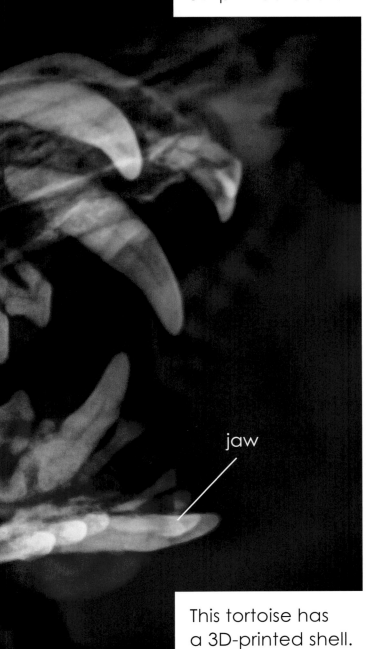

jaw

This tortoise has a 3D-printed shell.

shell

tortoise

▶ WATCH!

Watch the video (see page 32).
Watch the video (see page 32).
Can 3D printing help humans too?

Can you 3D print a house?

Some people 3D print houses. This house has lots of layers of earth!

wasp

This is a wasp's house. Wasps make their houses with layers, too.

earth

This is concrete. The 3D printer makes strong houses.

📋 PROJECT

Work with a friend. Draw a house to 3D print. Do you 3D print it with concrete, earth or chocolate?

Quiz

Choose the correct answers.

1 3D things are . . .

   a flat.

   b not flat.

2 3D printers make lots of . . .

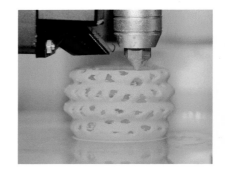

   a layers.

   b computers.

3 Doctors can 3D print . . . teeth.

   a old

   b new

4 This . . . has a
3D-printed beak.

   a bird

   b dog

5 . . . make their houses
with layers, too.

   a Wasps

   b Ants

DO YOU KNOW?

Visit **www.ladybirdeducation.co.uk** for
FREE **DO YOU KNOW?** teaching resources.

- video clips with simplified voiceover and subtitles
- video and comprehension activities
- class projects and lesson plans
- audio recording of every book
- digital version of every book
- full answer keys

To access video clips, audio tracks and digital books:

1 Go to **www.ladybirdeducation.co.uk**
2 Click 'Unlock book'
3 Enter the code below

C8uXzu0sD6

Stay safe online! Some of the DO YOU KNOW? activities ask children to do extra research online. Remember:

- ensure an adult is supervising;
- use established search engines such as Google or Kiddle;
- children should never share personal details, such as name, home or school address, telephone number or photos.

DO YOU KNOW?

Level 2

MAKING COMPUTERS

Written by Adékúnmi Olátúnjí
Series Editor: Nick Coates
Designed by Dynamo Limited

LADYBIRD BOOKS

UK | USA | Canada | Ireland | Australia
India | New Zealand | South Africa

Ladybird Books Ltd is part of the Penguin Random House group of companies
whose addresses can be found at global.penguinrandomhouse.com.
www.penguin.co.uk   www.puffin.co.uk   www.ladybird.co.uk

Penguin
Random House
UK

First published 2022
001

Image on cover (computer processor) copyright © Vierra/Shutterstock.com
image on page 1 (engineer) copyright © SeventyFour/Shutterstock.com
image on page 4 (calculator) copyright © J.Natayo/Shutterstock.com
image on page 4 (difficult) copyright © Carballo/Shutterstock.com
image on page 4 (electronic) copyright © Raigvi/Shutterstock.com
image on page 4 (expensive) copyright © ESB Professional/Shutterstock.com
image on page 4 (information) copyright © Rootstock/Shutterstock.com
image on page 4 (instructions) copyright © Myboys.me/Shutterstock.com
image on page 5 (machine) copyright © Gilmanshin/Shutterstock.com
image on page 5 (maths) copyright © R. Mackay Photography LLC/Shutterstock.com
image on page 5 (monitor) copyright © Freedom Life/Shutterstock.com
image on page 5 (recycle) copyright © RTimages/Shutterstock.com
image on page 5 (scientist) copyright © Aslysun/Shutterstock.com
image on page 5 (square) copyright © Penguin Random House
image on page 6 (traffic lights) copyright © Luis Santos/Shutterstock.com
image on page 6 and 7 (monitor) copyright © Africa Studio/Shutterstock.com
image on page 7 (washing machine) copyright © Macrovector/Shutterstock.com
image on page 7 (mobile phone) copyright © Wayhome Studio/Shutterstock.com
image on page 8 (ancient computer) copyright © Have Camera Will Travel/Alamy
image on page 8 and 9 (abacus) copyright © Akemaster/Shutterstock.com
image on page 9 (Eniac) copyright © Granger/Alamy
image on page 10 and 11 (Analytical Engine) copyright © Granger/Alamy
image on page 11 (Charles Babbage) copyright © Zip Lexing/Alamy
image on page 11 (Ada Lovelace) copyright © Pictorial Press Ltd/Alamy
image on page 12 (Baby Computer) copyright © John B Hewitt/Shutterstock.com
image on page 12 and 13 (Mark I) copyright © RBM Vintage Images/Alamy
image on page 14 (Apple computer) copyright © Maria Kray/Shutterstock.com
image on page 14 and 15 (retro computer) copyright © Twin Design/Shutterstock.com
image on page 15 (Microsoft) copyright © Twin Design/Shutterstock.com
image on page 15 (devices) copyright © Lumen-Digital/Shutterstock.com
image on page 16 and 17 (motherboard) copyright © Unkas Photo/Shutterstock.com

image on page 17 (microphone) copyright © Voljurij/Shutterstock.com
image on page 17 (keyboard and mouse) copyright © Gemini62/Shutterstock.com
image on page 17 (web camera) copyright © Volodymyr Krasyuk/Shutterstock.com
image on page 17 (monitor speakers) copyright © Aeolos Image/Shutterstock.com
image on page 17 (printer) copyright © Borriss.67/Shutterstock.com
image on page 18 and 19 (inside a computer) copyright © Kitch Bain/Shutterstock.com
image on page 19 (memory card) copyright © Oasishifi/Shutterstock.com
image on page 19 (computer processor) copyright © Vierra/Shutterstock.com
image on page 20 (pixels) copyright © Onur Cem/Shutterstock.com
image on page 20 and 21 (pixelated image) copyright © Prostock-studio/Shutterstock.com
image on page 21 (RGB) copyright © MicroOne/Shutterstock.com
image on page 22 (binary code) copyright © Jason Winter/Shutterstock.com
image on page 22 and 23 (abstract programmer) copyright © Metamorworks/Shutterstock.com
image on page 23 (decimal binary) copyright © Penguin Random House
image on page 24 and 25 (supercomputer) copyright © Dr Manager/Shutterstock.com
image on page 25 (engineer) copyright © SeventyFour/Shutterstock.com
image on page 25 (Fugaku) copyright © Dai Kurokawa, EPA-EFE/Shutterstock.com
image on page 26 (carrying computer shell) copyright © Aline Tong/Shutterstock.com
image on page 26 and 27 (landfill) copyright © Morten B/Shutterstock.com
image on page 27 (repair) copyright © Pearl Photo Pix/Shutterstock.com
image on page 28 (voice assistant) copyright © Best For Best/Shutterstock.com
image on page 28 and 29 (thinking teen) copyright © Roman Samborskyi/Shutterstock.com
image on page 29 (thinking robot) copyright © Phonlamai Photo/Shutterstock.com
image on page 30 (abacus) copyright © Akemaster/Shutterstock.com
image on page 30 (Analytical Engine) copyright © Granger/Shutterstock.com
image on page 30 (pixels) copyright © Onur Cem/Shutterstock.com
image on page 30 (binary code) copyright © Jason Winter/Shutterstock.com
image on page 31 (supercomputer) copyright © Dr Manager/Shutterstock.com
image on page 31 (Fugaku) copyright © Dai Kurokawa, EPA-EFE/Shutterstock.com
image on page 31 (voice assistant) copyright © Best For Best/Shutterstock.com
image on page 31 (thinking teen) copyright © Roman Samborskyi/Shutterstock.com

Printed in China

The authorized representative in the EEA is Penguin Random House Ireland,
Morrison Chambers, 32 Nassau Street, Dublin D02 YH68

A CIP catalogue record for this book is available from the British Library

ISBN: 978-0-241-55944-4

All correspondence to:
Ladybird Books
Penguin Random House Children's
One Embassy Gardens, 8 Viaduct Gardens, London SW11 7BW

Contents

New words

calculator

difficult

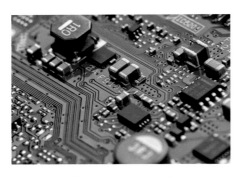

electronic

expensive

information

instruction

machine

maths

monitor
(noun)

recycle

scientist

square

What is a computer?

A computer is a clever **machine**. It helps us to do different things.

traffic light

A computer can change a traffic light from red to orange, and then to green.

There are computers inside washing machines. They start and stop the washing machines.

washing machine

The computer in your mobile phone does lots of things!

mobile phone

 **THINK!**

Think about which things in your home have computers inside them.

What were the first computers?

The first computers were **calculators**. They helped people to do **maths**.

Some people think the first calculator in the world was the abacus.

This computer is very old. **Scientists** think it shows days, months and years.

This is the first **electronic** computer in 1946. It was a very big computer!

abacus

Work with a friend. Find out how to do maths on an abacus.

9

Who were Charles Babbage and Ada Lovelace?

Charles Babbage was an English scientist in the 1800s. He wanted to answer **difficult** maths questions with a machine.

His famous machine was the Analytical Engine.

But Charles Babbage did not make the Analytical Engine. It was very **expensive.**

Analytical Engine

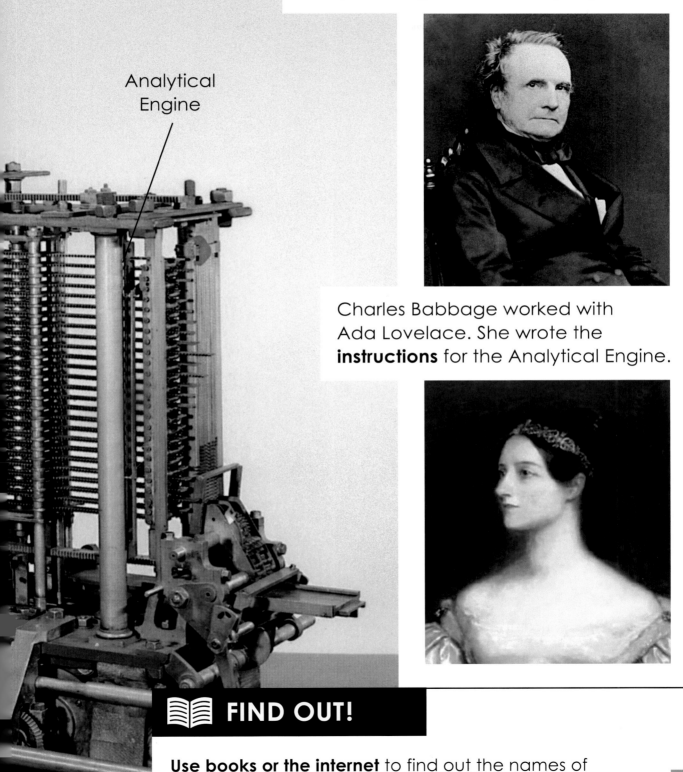

Charles Babbage worked with Ada Lovelace. She wrote the **instructions** for the Analytical Engine.

📖 **FIND OUT!**

Use books or the internet to find out the names of other machines Charles Babbage wanted to make.

How big were the first computers?

Old computers were big because all the parts inside the computer were big.

The first computers were very big.
Sometimes, scientists put
computers in big rooms!

This computer is called
the Harvard Mark I.
It has 765,000 parts!

▶ WATCH!

Watch the video (see page 32).
Which old computer was the biggest.

When did computers come into our homes?

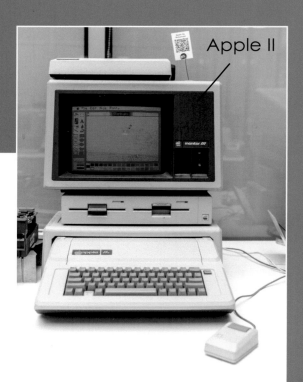

Apple II

Apple made one of the first personal computers in 1977.

The old computers were big and very expensive. People did not have them in their homes. The first small computers in homes were in the 1970s.

Microsoft made Windows in 1985.

desktop

tablet

laptop

Now, many homes have
lots of personal computers.

THINK!

Do you have a personal computer at home?
Do you have more than one?
How many do you have?

What are the parts of a computer?

Computers have many parts. One part is the motherboard.

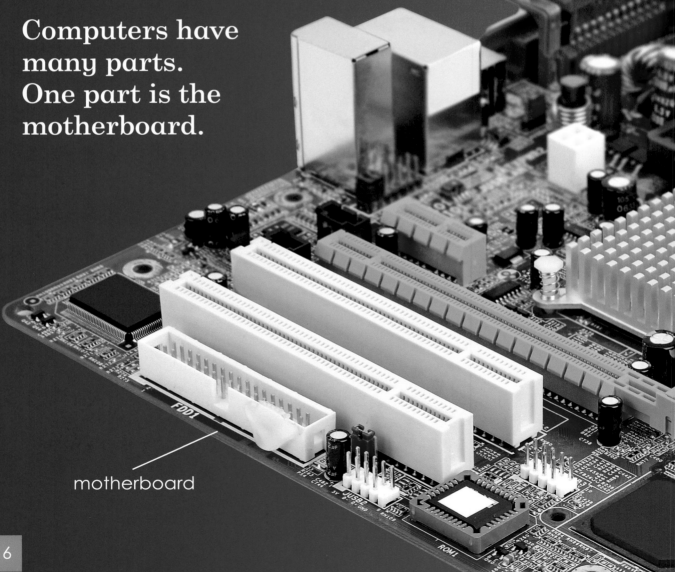

motherboard

All the parts of the computer meet on the motherboard.

These parts take **information** into a computer.

camera

microphone

keyboard

mouse

speaker

monitor

printer

These parts send information from the computer.

🔍 LOOK!

Look at the pages. How does the computer give us information?

Two important parts inside every computer are the memory card and the processor.

The memory card remembers the instructions.

The processor reads the instructions. Then it tells the other parts of the computer what to do.

 **WATCH!**

Watch the video (see page 32).
What other parts can a computer have?

What is **red, green and blue?**

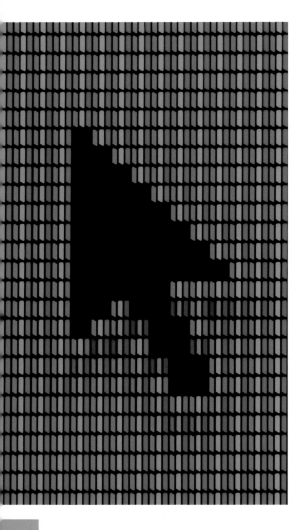

We make pictures on computer **monitors** with very small **squares**. We call these squares pixels.

Each pixel has a colour.

pixel

Pixels are red, green or blue. These three colours together can make new colours.

🔍 LOOK!

Look at the pages. Which colours can you make with red, green and blue?

21

What is binary?

Binary is the language computers speak.
It has two numbers . . . and no letters!
Binary numbers are 0 and 1.
There are no other numbers in binary.

```
10110111110001110100010111
10001011110100010111011011 0
11011000101110100010111101 1
10100100001010101101111 10
0101110001101110001011 10
101111101011101111011000101
011011011110111000101111 0
110001011101011101100010 1
0111011011010111101001000 00
00101111011101101011100010
101101111001101101111101 01
```

Instructions for computers are in binary because
computers can only understand 0s and 1s.

22

We can write all numbers in binary.

DECIMAL	BINARY
0	0
1	1
2	10
3	11
4	100
5	101
6	110
7	111
8	1000
9	1001
10	1010

📋 PROJECT

Work with a friend. What is the number 11 in binary?
What is the number 260 in binary?

What are supercomputers?

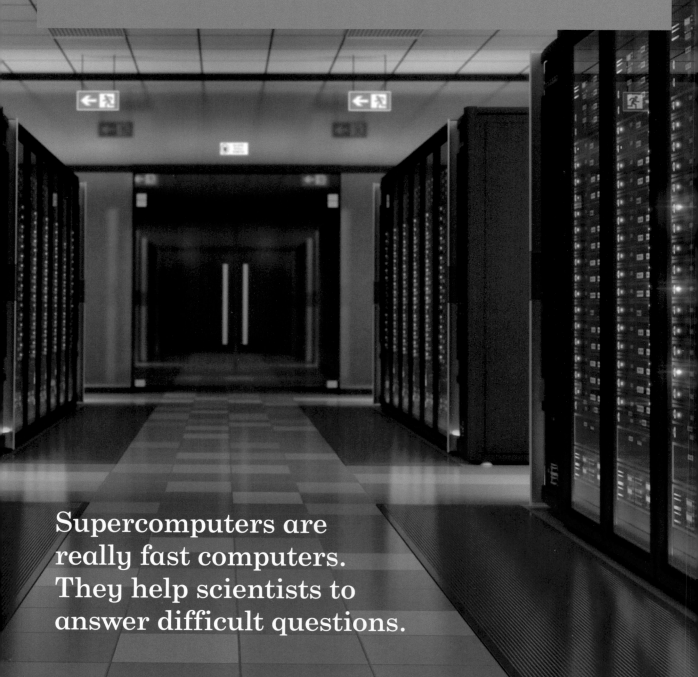

Supercomputers are really fast computers. They help scientists to answer difficult questions.

Supercomputers are very big. They can work with lots of information.

The Fujitsu Fugaku is a very big supercomputer in Japan. It tells us about the weather.

📖 FIND OUT!

Use books or the internet to find out what questions supercomputers can answer now.

Can you recycle computers?

Landfills are bad for people. They are bad for the water, environment and animals, too.

You can **recycle** most parts of a computer. But a lot of old computers go to landfills.

landfill

Old computer parts can make new things. You can also give your old computers to other people.

▶ **WATCH!**

Watch the video (see page 32). What do people make with old computer parts?

Can computers think?

People give instructions to computers. The instructions tell the computers what to do.

VOICE ASSISTANT

Today, some computers can listen and say words. They can answer the questions you ask. But they cannot talk like people do.

28

Computers can understand instructions and remember a lot of information, but they cannot think like people do.

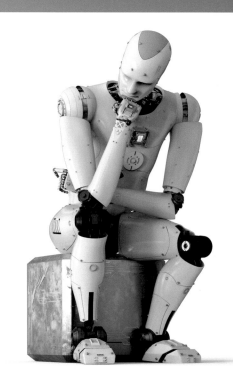

 PROJECT

Work with a friend. Write questions you think a computer cannot answer.

Quiz

Choose the correct answers.

1 The first computer was . . .

   a a calculator.

   b an abacus.

   c a personal computer.

2 Who wrote the instructions for the Analytical Engine?

   a Charles Lovelace

   b Charles Babbage

   c Ada Lovelace

3 Which colours do pixels have?

   a red, blue and green

   b black, white and red

   c red, blue and yellow

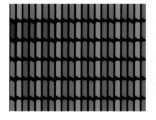

4 Which numbers are in binary?

   a 0 and 1

   b 1 and 2

   c 0, 1 and 2

5 Supercomputers can . . .
  a help scientists.
  b have a conversation.
  c make you food.

6 Fujitsu Fugaku is a supercomputer that tells us about . . .
  a the time.
  b the weather.
  c Japan.

7 Computers can . . .
  a feel happy.
  b listen and say words.
  c eat cake.

8 People give . . . to computers.
  a instructions
  b food
  c hugs

DO YOU KNOW?

Visit www.ladybirdeducation.co.uk for
FREE **DO YOU KNOW?** teaching resources.

- video clips with simplified voiceover and subtitles
- video and comprehension activities
- class projects and lesson plans
- audio recording of every book
- digital version of every book
- full answer keys

To access video clips, audio tracks and digital books:

1 Go to **www.ladybirdeducation.co.uk**
2 Click 'Unlock book'
3 Enter the code below

hVnrqKc50F

Stay safe online! Some of the DO YOU KNOW? activities ask children to do extra research online. Remember:

- ensure an adult is supervising;
- use established search engines such as Google or Kiddle;
- children should never share personal details, such as name, home or school address, telephone number or photos.